B48 359 926 8

D0717767

The Defeat of the
Spanish Armada

Deborah Fox

H www.heinemann.co.uk/library
Visit our website to find out more information about Heinemann Library books.

To order:
☎ Phone 44 (0) 1865 888066
📄 Send a fax to 44 (0) 1865 314091
💻 Visit the Heinemann Bookshop at www.heinemann.co.uk/library to browse our catalogue and order online.

First published in Great Britain by Heinemann Library, Halley Court, Jordan Hill, Oxford OX2 8EJ, a division of Reed Educational and Professional Publishing Ltd. Heinemann is a registered trademark of Reed Educational & Professional Publishing Ltd.

OXFORD MELBOURNE AUCKLAND JOHANNESBURG BLANTYRE
GABORONE IBADAN PORTSMOUTH (NH) USA CHICAGO

Designed by Joanna Hinton-Malivoire
Illustrations by Peter Bull Art Studio
Originated by Repro Multi Warna
Printed by South China Printing Company, Hong Kong/China

ISBN 0 431 12333 0
06 05 04 03 02
10 9 8 7 6 5 4 3 2 1

British Library Cataloguing in Publication Data
Fox, Deborah
How do we know about the defeat of the Spanish Armada?
1.Armada, 1588 - Juvenile literature
I.Title II. The defeat of the Spanish Armada
942'.055

Acknowledgements
The Publishers would like to thank the following for permission to reproduce photographs: Fotomas: p23; Hulton: p22; Magdalene College, Cambridge: p24; National Maritime Museum: pp5, 21; Ossie Palmer: p4; The Art Archive: pp20, 25; Ulster Museum: pp26, 27.

Cover photograph reproduced with permission of AKG.

Words printed in **bold letters like these** are explained in the Glossary

Contents

England and Spain

This statue is of Sir Francis Drake. He was born in Devon in about 1539. He was a great sailor who fought in sea battles against the enemies of England. One of England's enemies was Spain.

King Philip of Spain was a **Catholic.**
He was very angry that Elizabeth I,
the **Protestant** Queen of England,
was helping other countries to fight
against Spain.

Philip prepares for war

In 1585 King Philip started to prepare for war against England. His shipbuilders began to build an **armada** of new warships. The English heard about what the Spanish were doing.

In April 1587 Sir Francis Drake found out that some Spanish ships were in Cadiz in Spain. In a surprise attack, his **fleet** swept into the **harbour** and sank 30 Spanish **galleons**.

The Armada sets sail

Philip had wanted the **Armada** to
attack England that year, but it was
July 1588 when the Armada set sail.
The **commander** was the Duke of
Medina-Sidonia. A week later he
and his crew spied land.

Beacons were lit along the south coast of England to warn the people that the Armada had arrived. The English sailors planned to set sail later that night when the wind was right.

The English fleet

That night the English ships set sail.
Their **commander** was Lord Howard
of Effingham. He worked well with
Sir Francis Drake and his other captains.

For days the English ships chased the **Armada**, but they couldn't get close. The Spanish ships kept in the shape of a **crescent**, with the largest **galleons** at the edges to frighten their enemy.

The surprise attack

The Duke headed for Calais in France. More ships were going to meet him there. The English decided to attack. They set fire to eight of their own ships and sent them towards the Spanish.

The Duke had expected an attack, but his sailors panicked. They cut their anchor ropes and scattered to avoid the burning ships. The Spanish **fleet** was now separated.

Battle at sea

The English swept in to attack the **Armada** the next morning. The Spanish ships were huge and had more **cannons**, but the English ships were swifter and their cannons were better.

After hours of fighting, the Spanish were losing. Their battered ships began to drift towards the rocks. Suddenly the wind changed direction and the Spanish ships were able to escape.

The Queen visits her troops

Queen Elizabeth was worried that the Spanish might return. She wanted to make sure her army was ready for battle. On 9 August she gave a wonderful speech to her soldiers.

Over a week passed and the Spanish
still had not made another attack.
Elizabeth decided that her troops
could go home.

The dangerous seas

While the Queen was visiting her troops, the Spanish ships were battling against fierce weather. Ships were wrecked in the stormy seas and many soldiers and sailors died.

England's victory was celebrated throughout the land. They had lost ships, but it was much worse for the Spanish. They had lost about 20,000 men and half their ships.

How do we know?

To celebrate the English victory, artists showed what had happened. This **tapestry** was woven in 1588 to show the defeat of the Spanish **Armada**.

This medallion was made to celebrate the English victory. It is now in the National Maritime Museum in London.

Cards and letters

Playing cards celebrated the English victory. These ones have survived for over 400 years.

This letter was signed by Lord Howard and all his captains. They made a promise to drive the Spanish from England's shores.

Maps

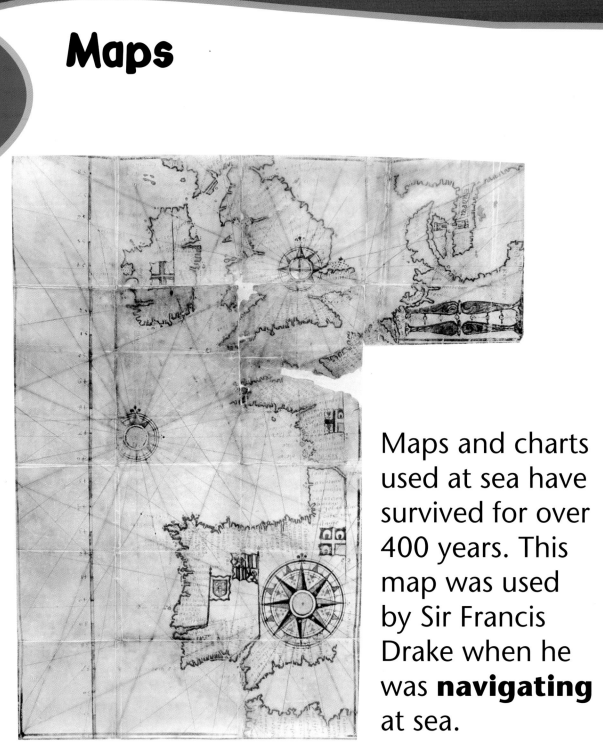

Maps and charts used at sea have survived for over 400 years. This map was used by Sir Francis Drake when he was **navigating** at sea.

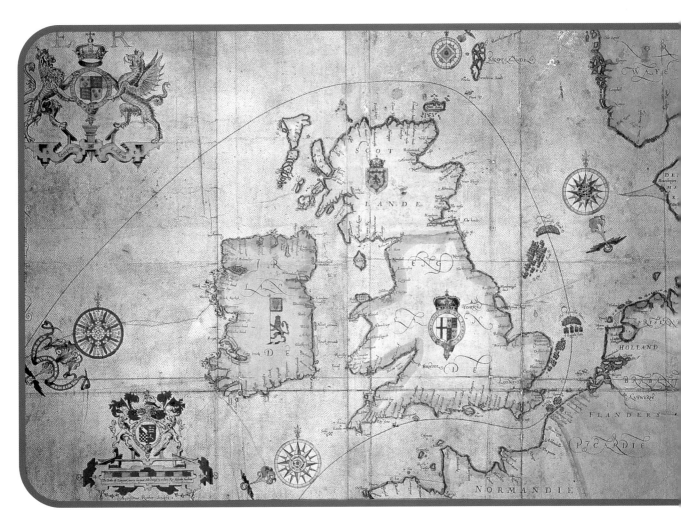

This map of the British Isles shows the course King Philip's **Armada** took to get back to Spain.

Weapons and wreckage

When ships sink, **wreckage** is often washed up on the shore. This **cannon** is from one of the Spanish **galleons**, the *Trinidad Valencera*.

People who were sailing on the Spanish ships often carried their jewels and gold. This gold cross is in the Ulster Museum in Belfast. It came from the ship *Girona*.

Timeline

1585 King Philip II of Spain gives orders for ships to be built for his **Armada**.

19 April 1587 Sir Francis Drake attacks Spanish ships in Cadiz **harbour**.

19 July 1588 The Spanish spy English land.

20 July 1588 English ships follow the Armada and try to attack.

27 July 1588 The Duke of Medina-Sidonia anchors off Calais.

28 July 1588 Lord Howard sends in eight blazing fireships. The Spanish scatter.

29 July 1588 The Armada is attacked by the English and flees north.

9 August 1588 Queen Elizabeth gives her famous speech to her soldiers in Tilbury.

17 August 1588 The Queen gives orders for her army to go home.

September 1588 Many Spanish ships are wrecked off the coast of Ireland.

October 1588 The Duke of Medina-Sidonia arrives back in Spain.

Biographies

Lord Charles Howard of Effingham

Lord Charles Howard of Effingham was born in 1536. He was a cousin of Queen Elizabeth I. He was made the Lord High Admiral of the English **fleet** and led it to victory over the Armada. He died in 1624.

Sir Francis Drake

Sir Francis Drake was born around 1539 at a farm near Tavistock. He learned about ships when he was an **apprentice** to a shipmaster. In 1577 he was the first Englishman to sail around the world. He served under Lord Howard as Vice Admiral of the English fleet. He died in 1596.

The Duke of Medina-Sidonia

The Duke of Medina-Sidonia was born in 1550 into a rich family in Spain. The Duke blamed himself for the defeat of the Armada. The King of Spain did not and continued to give him positions of power. The Duke died in 1619.

Glossary

apprentice someone who goes to work for a skilled person in order to learn how to do the job

Armada a large number of ships

beacon a fire or light on a hill. It is usually lit to warn of an invasion.

cannon a large heavy gun

Catholic a Christian who belongs to the Roman Catholic Church. The Pope is the Head of this Church.

commander person who leads others in war

crescent curved shape

fleet all the warships of a country

galleons large sailing ships with three or more masts

harbour an area of water where ships can be anchored

navigate to plan the way the ship will go

Protestant a Christian who does not belong to the Roman Catholic Church. Protestants separated from the Catholic Church many years ago to set up their own Church.

tapestry a heavy piece of material that often hangs on a wall. On it is a picture or pattern that has been woven with threads or wool.

wreckage the bits that are left after something has been destroyed

Further reading

Lives and Times: Queen Elizabeth I, Rachael Bell, Heinemann Library, 1998

You may need help to read this book:
History of Britain topic books: The Spanish Armada, Brian Williams, Heinemann Library, 1995

Index

Titles in the *How do we know about ...?* series include:

How do we know about ...?
The Defeat of the
Spanish Armada

Hardback   0 431 12333 0

How do we know about ...?
The
Great Fire of London

Hardback   0 431 12331 4

How do we know about ...?
The
Great Plague

Hardback   0 431 12332 2

How do we know about ...?
The
Gunpowder Plot

Hardback   0 431 12330 6

Find out about the other titles in this series on our website www.heinemann.co.uk/library